COLOR TEST PAGE

Also by Debra Webb Rogers:

Non-fiction

The Boone Connection in the Lost Counties
San Marco
Jacksonville's Southside
Dancing Between the Ears
Choosing A Dance School, What Every Parent Should Consider

Fiction
(Writing as Violet Rightmire)

Dancing in Time
A Windfall Christmas

Family Tree Coloring Book
Thacker House Enterprises August 2016
Copyright©2016 by Debra Webb Rogers
ISBN 978-0-980-1919-4-3

Thacker House Enterprises

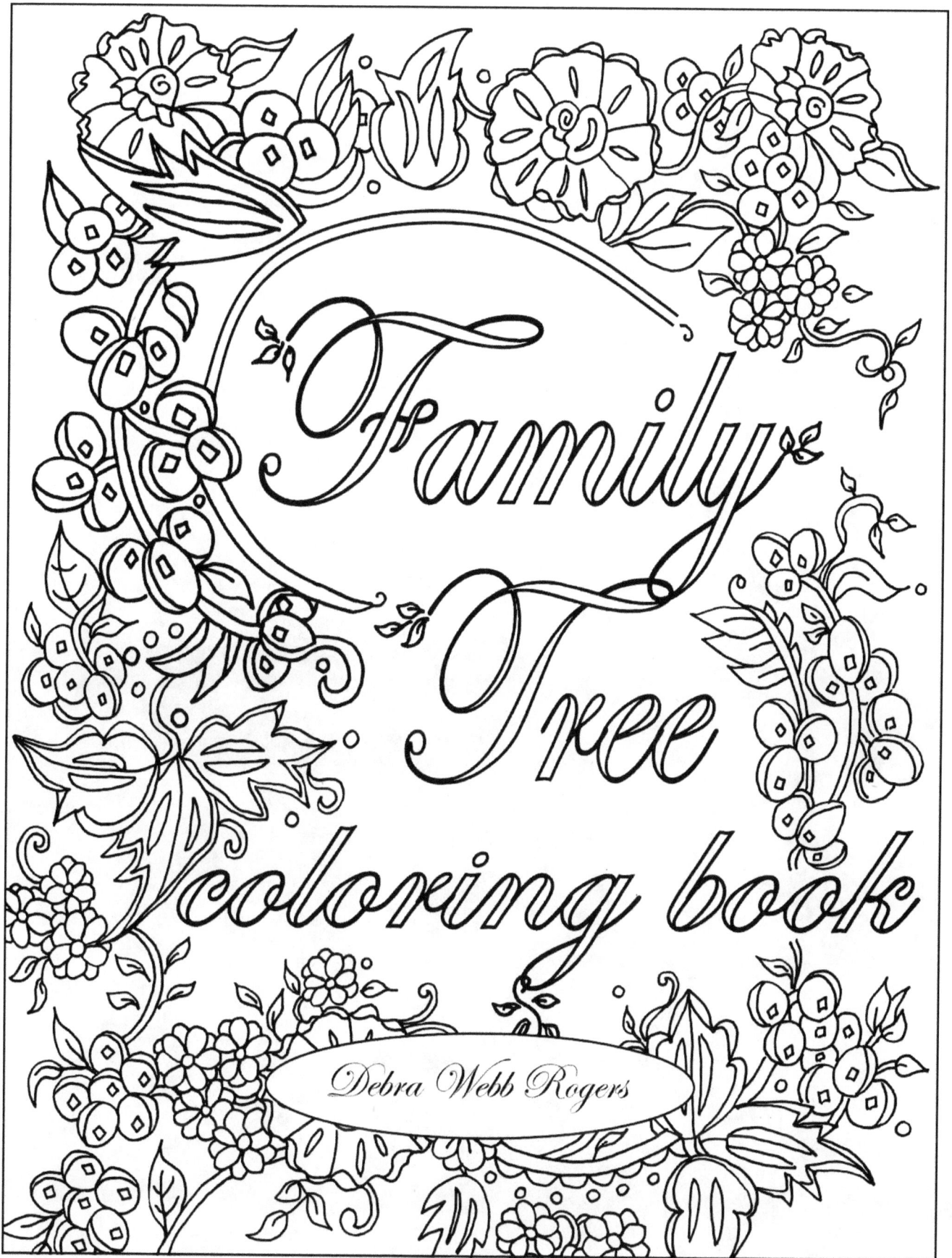

Family Tree coloring book

Debra Webb Rogers

TABLE OF CONTENTS

Tips and Ideas

Put an extra piece of paper behind the coloring page. This makes the pen or colored pencil move smoothly and prevents any color or impressions from being transferred to the following page.

Write any genealogical information on a scrap piece of paper before writing it on the coloring page. This ensures accuracy in the data.

Colors can be assigned to the text for each category, like green for Parents, or yellow for Grandparents, etc.; thus color-coding the data.

Completed pages can be removed and framed, put in a scrap book, or placed in plastic sleeves and compiled with family photos into an extensive genealogical record.

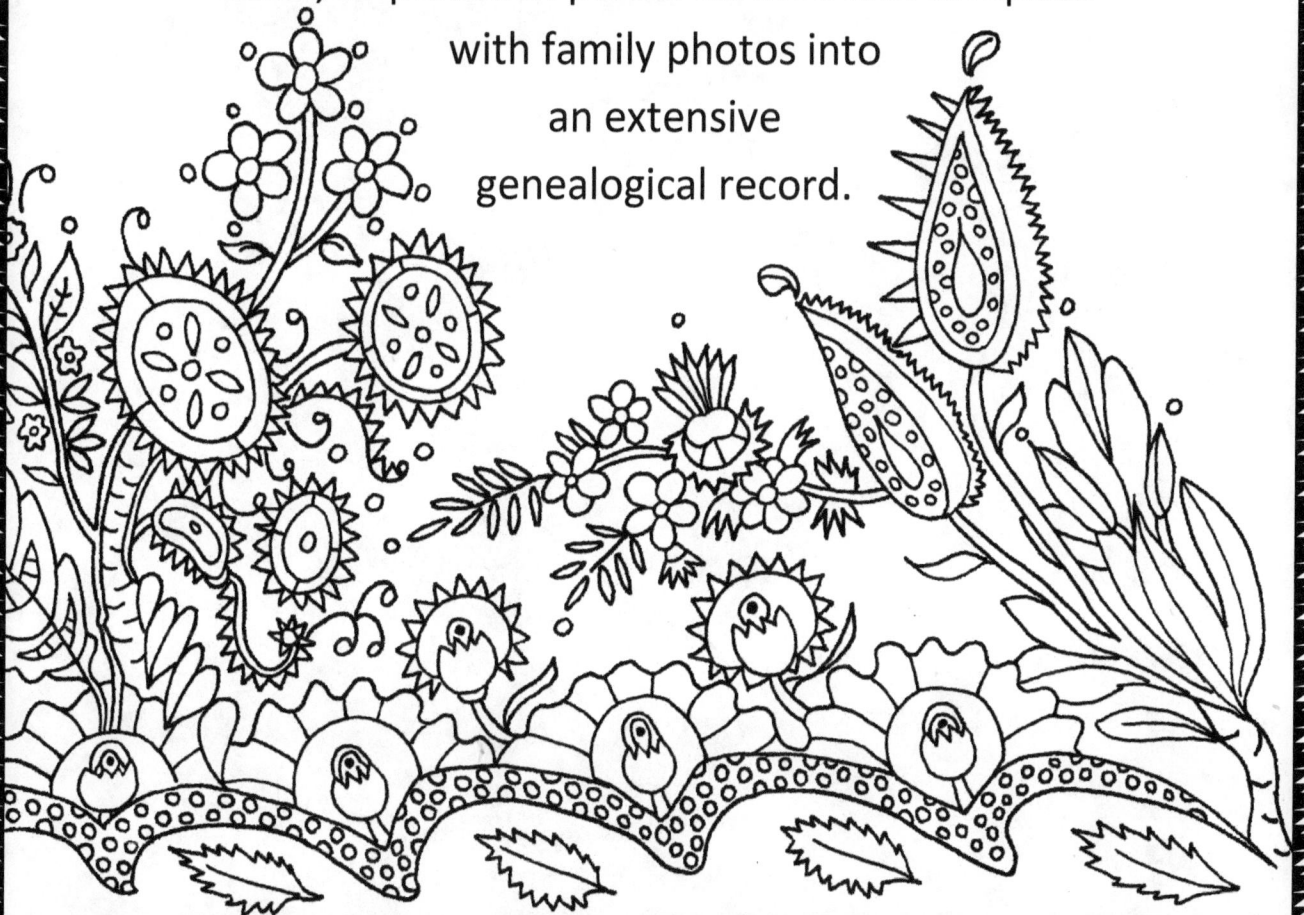

THIS BOOK IS THE

FAMILY TREE
RECORD
OF

Birthdate:

Where:

MY SPOUSE

Marriage

Date: _____

Place: _____

Our Children

MY PARENTS

Father

_____
_____
_____

Mother

_____
_____

My Siblings

_____

_____

_____

_____

_____

_____

_____

_____

_____

_____

_____

_____

_____

_____

MY
MOTHER'S
ANCESTORS

20

MY MOTHER'S PARENTS

Father	Mother
_____	_____
_____	_____
_____	_____
_____	_____
_____	_____

MARRIAGE DATE & LOCATION:

_____

MY MOTHER'S SIBLINGS

_____

_____

_____

_____

_____

_____

_____

MY MOTHER'S MATERNAL GRANDPARENTS

Grandmother:

_____

Born: _____

Died: _____

Grandfather:

_____

Born: _____

Died: _____

Married:

Date: _____

Place: _____

MY MOTHER'S PATERNAL GRANDPARENTS

Grandmother:

_____

Born: _____

Died: _____

Grandfather:

_____

Born: _____

Died: _____

Married:

Date: _____

Place: _____

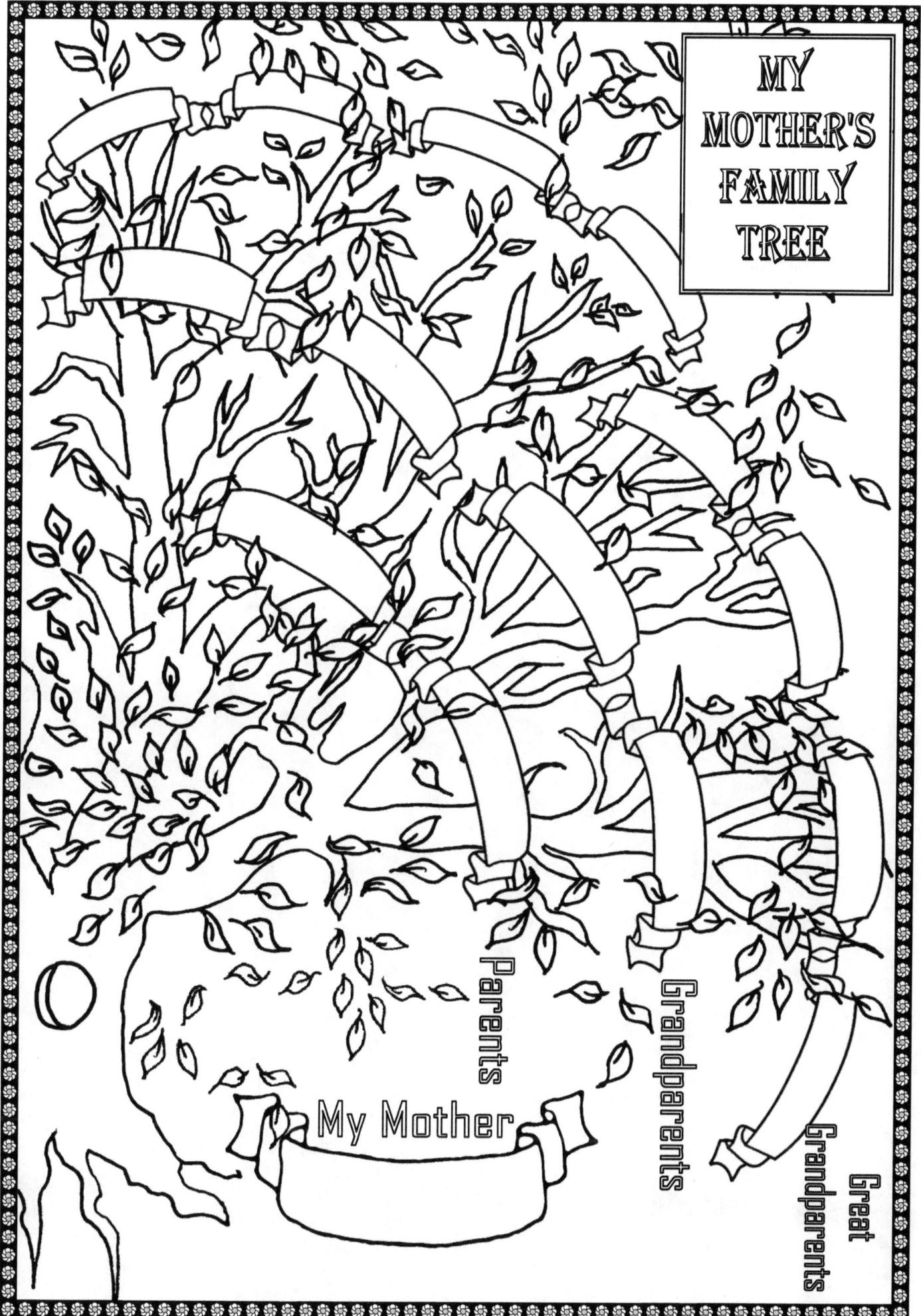

MY MOTHER'S FAMILY TREE

My Mother

Parents

Grandparents

Great Grandparents

Notes

MY
FATHER'S
ANCESTORS

MY FATHER'S PARENTS

Mother: _____

_____

_____

Father: _____

_____

_____

Married: _____

_____

MY
FATHER'S SIBLINGS

_____

_____

_____

_____

_____

_____

_____

_____

_____

_____

_____

_____

_____

_____

MY FATHER'S MATERNAL GRANDPARENTS

Grandmother _____

Born: _____

Died: _____

Grandfather _____

Born: _____

Died: _____

Marriage:

Date: _____

Place: _____

MY FATHER'S
PATERNAL GRANDPARENTS

Grandmother: _____

Born: _____
Died: _____

Grandfather: _____

Born: _____
Died: _____

Married:

Date: _____
Place: _____

Father

Parents

Grand-
parents

Great
Grandparents

MY
FATHER'S
FAMILY
TREE

NOTES

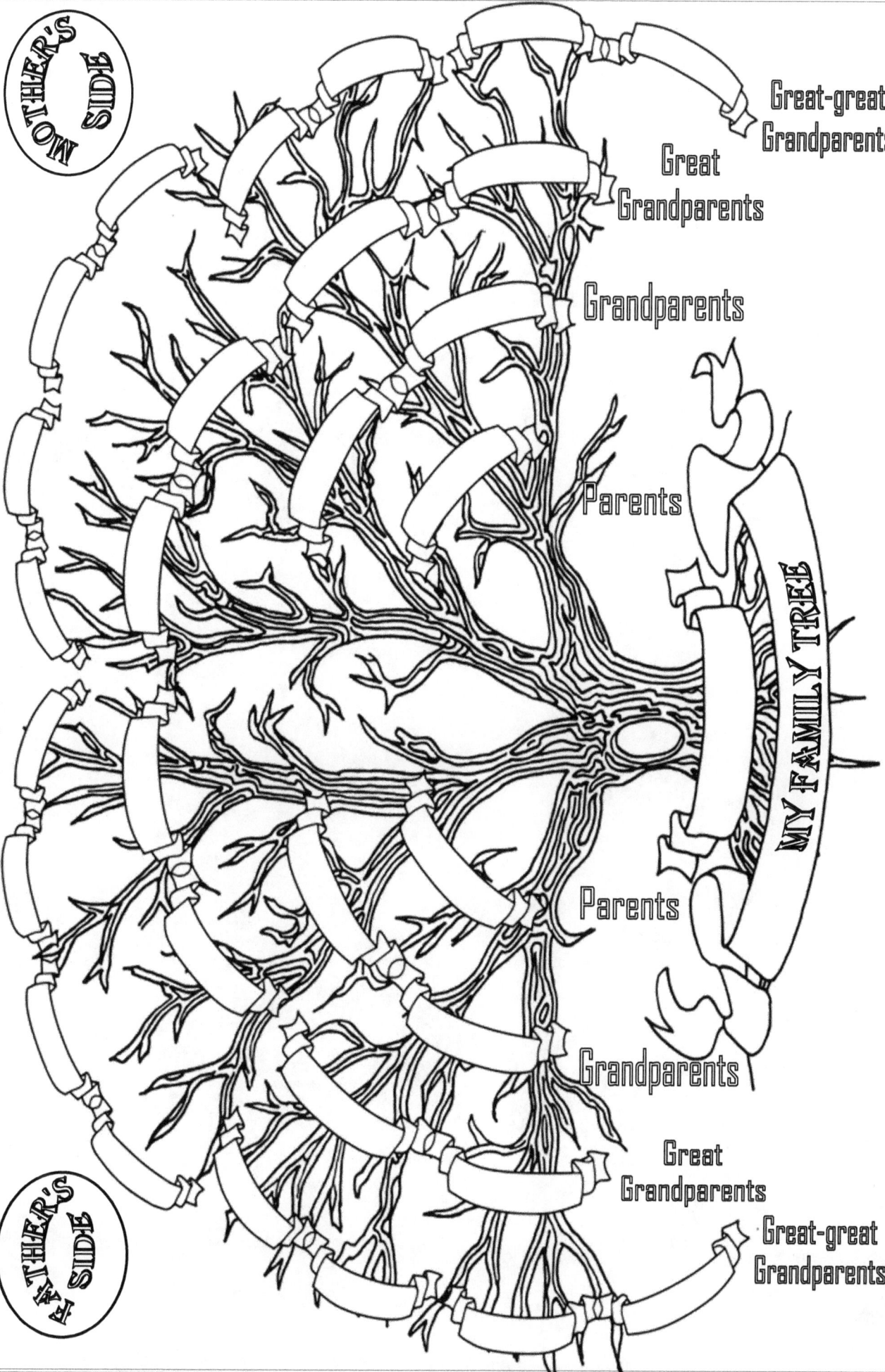

Great-great
Grandparents

Great
Grandparents

Grandparents

Parents

MY FAMILY TREE

Parents

Grandparents

Great
Grandparents

Great-great
Grandparents

www.ingramcontent.com/pod-product-compliance
Lightning Source LLC
Chambersburg PA
CBHW051346290326
41933CB00042B/3306